Run & Shoot Management

Creating
Managerial Excitement
and Growth with
Generation X

by
Don Boone, MSW
Donna Boone Martin, MBA
Daniel B. Martin, III

Publisher: Ralph Roberts

Vice President/Publishing: Pat Hutchison Roberts

Cover Design: Gayle Graham

Senior Editor: Barbara Blood

Editors: Susan Parker, Laura Cox

Interior Design and Electronic Page Assembly: **WorldComm**®

Printed in the United States of America.

10 9 8 7 6 5 4 3

ISBN 1-56664-132-2

WorldComm®—a division of Creativity, Inc.–is a full-service publisher located at 65 Macedonia Road, Alexander NC 28701. Phone (828) 252-9515 or (828) 255-8719 fax.

WorldComm® is distributed to the trade by **Alexander Distributing**, 65 Macedonia Road, Alexander NC 28701. Phone (828) 252-9515 or (828) 255-8719 fax. For orders only: 1-800-472-0438. Visa and MasterCard accepted.

This book is also available on the internet in the **Publishers CyberMall**. Set your browser to http://www.abooks.com and enjoy the many fine values available there.

Contents

For Additional Information:

MANAGEMENT
CONSULTANTS

16 Spears Ave. #2
Asheville, N.C. 28801
Phone (828) 258-0905
Fax (828) 252-6294

Introduction

Gone are the days when the manager could feel comfortable and confident that a proven management style, exercised with intensity and discipline would yield operational and organizational success. Technological changes, short product life cycles and our dynamic culture create and make obsolete markets, industries, processes and employees with ever increasing rapidity. Change and uncertainty are the only constants, yet, opportunities for achievement and excitement have never been greater for managers.

There is a scarcity of employees. In addition, there is a constantly changing demand for the type of employees needed and for the duration of the need. Possibly the most constant feature in the employee situation is that the available employees have few leverage points or "hot buttons" and that they too, are in a constant state of evolution. Management today is not unlike trying to putt in the rain - with the player, the ball and the green all in movement.

One bright light, however, is the potential of those in Generation X. Born in the sixties and seventies, this employee group is likely the brightest, best educated and most informed of any similar group in history. Bringing this groups' potential to fruition places more demands upon management than any other group has in history. They show little automatic, or unearned respect for conventional establishment values or traditional motivators.

Managing the Generation X employee successfully, while finding meaning, excitement and self-actualization through the experience is the focus of this book.

I

Different Creatures Require Different Care and Feeding

ISSUES COVERED IN THIS CHAPTER:

- ♦ **Different Strokes For Different Folks.**
- ♦ **Xers Respond To Challenge, Growth New Experience And Risk.**
- ♦ **Cats Cannot Be Herded — We Must Lead The Xer.**
- ♦ **Enlightened Leadership Yields New Levels Of Productivity.**
- ♦ **"Work Should Be More Fun Than Fun", Coward.**
- ♦ **There Is Passion And There Is Apathy. Passion Is Better.**
- ♦ **Motivate By Raising The Bar — *NEVER* By Lowering It.**
- ♦ **Influence And Respect Must Be Earned.**

Off to the Peace Corps

Those reared in one era will seek security. In another, risk and opportunity will be sought after the basic self-actualization. Baby boomers seem to have a very material focus and may sacrifice quality of life and freedom to obtain them. Just the opposite is true of those belonging to Generation X. Freedom, quality of life and a variety of experiences are the primary focus of this group. The Xers may enjoy all of the above, but they are remarkably free of their control.

Having known more affluence, freedom and enlightenment than discipline, the Xer with a good job, excellent benefits and a promising future is capable of resigning to take a steamer trip around the world. This choice is beyond the comprehension of the young lady's parents, employers and most of the community. After all that was invested in education, training and establishing social values, the decision is seen as irrational and irresponsible. The member of Generation X, or the Xer, has little trust in the establishment values or their ability to provide meaning for life.

Our society has an amazing creative ability to label this individuality with negative social connotations and even with medical diagnosis. The current society has relieved itself of the responsibility for dealing with the erratic behavior of the Xers by labeling some of it as Attention Deficit Disorder. Almost by definition, the label is said to be warranted when an individual can only attend for substantial periods of time to the tasks which they find interesting and stimulating. Most of us have had ADD symptoms in church, PTA, and afternoon math classes. Anyone not brain dead can find more meaning and adventure in exploring their own mental activity than enduring the rote and dull pronouncements of another.

Like it or not, much of the Generation X work population is borderline ADD. However, what is missing in the ability / willingness to attend to the mundane is returned in ability to give all to a function in which meaning, excitement, creation, and elitism and differentiation can be found. Those with children will remember the times when they were confronted with "we are bored, what can we do?" Those who manage Xers will be constantly confronted with the question in many different forms and will welcome the opportunity to provide a vision and leadership. Without managerial vision and leadership, chaos is not unlikely.

Generation X may well provide an impetus for quantum change in American management styles and effectiveness which will be the prototype for management in the 21st century. This provocation for change is likely of greater value and has a longer life expectancy than the manufacturing or service contribution of the Xers. These workers certainly have the potential to take management to a new level. The changing approaches will likely bring results similar to the "West Coast Offense" and the success seen in the "Run and Shoot".

The successful manager in the future will have to create an environment which is more rewarding and gives a better quality of life than almost all other options, including doing nothing at the beach, waiting tables at Aspen, going on welfare or moving in with the parents. Managers able to give up old conceptual paradigms, interact with and provide this rewarding experience for the Xers will have access to a valuable resource. They may be free spirited and not unlike interacting with creatures in the wild, but have so much untapped potential. Steve Spurrier, the successful football coach at the University of Florida, calls this a "Fun and Gun" system.

Noel Coward once wrote that "work should be more fun than fun." James Michener said it a little differently:

> *The master in the art of living makes little distinction between his work and his play, his labor and his leisure, his mind and his body, his information and his recreation, his love and his religion. He hardly knows which is which. He simply pursues his vision of excellence at whatever he does, leaving others to decide whether he is working or playing. To him, he's always doing both.*

Don Meridith once reflected on Monday Night Football that the game is so brutal that it will destroy you if you are not having fun. The Xers believe, live and practice all of this.

The comments by Coward, Meridith and Michener all suggest that the work can be rewarding and exciting. The authors of this book contend that with proper leadership, a little management and a lot of coaching, the common man can have the same experience as athletes. Professionals and artists can have it in the common workplace. The common work experience can invite the same passion shown in religion or in love. Without vision, the people perish. Without passion, it does not matter.

It would be less of a challenge if we could provide a simple training manual for those in Generation X and for those who choose to lead, manage and coach them. Fortunately, the challenge offers too great a reward to be accessed that easily. Man usually breaks old paradigms only when given no other choice. This is especially true when the magnitude of managerial and coaching changes will be similar to those brought about by the forward pass in basketball and the run and gun offense in football. The moving jump shot from outside the circle is a little different to relate to than that two hand set shot.

Kelly Johnson of Lockheed may be a good model. Steven Jobs did some of the same sorts of things at Apple Computer early in his career. The Black Sheep Squadron of WWII and later its television series also related to management capable of taking a diverse and difficult group and achieving extra ordinary results through the projection of an unique elitist vision which invited individual participation.

Meaning and excitement are very personal and come from the intensity of the individual's investment and not from the nature of the activity where the investment is placed. Through near obsession and personal investment, some find meaning and excitement from collecting match book covers, spitting watermelon seeds and even racing hospital beds.

Making widgets may never be exciting. How we make widgets, how many widgets we make, how our widgets are elitist widgets, how much fun we have making widgets and the relationships we develop while we make widgets is an entirely different matter. Therein lies the opportunity for extra ordinary performance and excellence.

· · NOTES · ·

II

We Succeed and Fail by Our Paradigms

ISSUES COVERED IN THIS CHAPTER:

- ◆ *Never try to stop the world to get on or off.*

- ◆ *Stable paradigms may well be the most restrictive prisons.*

- ◆ *Those who successfully interact with other paradigms become leaders.*

- ◆ *Competence and flexibility provide a longer life expectancy.*

- ◆ *It is not wise to walk backwards into the future.*

- ◆ *A business system or structure must enhance individual self-actualization if it is to endure.*

The most important determinants of organizational behavior are the leader's / coach's conceptual paradigms and the ability to model and communicate those paradigms. It takes both. The greatest of belief systems are of limited value unless they are demonstrated and communicated. Ineffectual systems never had a chance as they were flawed from the onset. The leader's paradigm also has to fit the situation. Therefore, our modern manager / coach has to have conceptual paradigms and model flexibility which are dynamic enough to maintain the essential elements in diverse environments.

Successful managers will have to constantly re-frame their own belief systems before being able to create a competitive vision and work experience for others. Most leaders / managers have gotten in their positions through discipline, hard work and the loyalty to the establishment and cultural values in their own comfort zone. After all, the society tends to teach the same restrictive paradigms to all levels and ages within the society. It is only a few of the well established that are able to break the hypnotic suggestions of past experience, create new ones and pass them on to others.

The Xers have been able to break away from the traditional establishment paradigm paralysis. They have not been able to replace them with a new and developing conceptual set. Therefore, the opportunity is exceptionally fertile for the gifted visionary capable of learning a different language. A language which can be

combined with his own and projected into an alloy more versatile than either component part.

Every individual, business and society has a tendency to maintain things as they are. While we may gripe, we love and relish the familiar, stable and especially the economic equilibrium as well as the pseudo security it offers. The illusion of predictability does reduce anxiety. This illusion also provides inordinate support to deteriorating comfort zones by denying intruding dangers and challenge. The illusion of security is a creation of man, or maybe the ostrich, and is not compatible with the changes of the real world. There are few comfort zones not vulnerable to illness, flood, volcano or the technological obsolescence of the product.

Industries, products, and processes have an increasingly shortened half life. Everything is happening and changing at an increasingly rapid pace. Most business activities and services are essentially obsolete by the time they are established or created. Future managerial leaders will welcome and lead the passages and transitions rather than resist them and cling to the familiar past lives of their business.

The Xers are more capable of the dynamic interaction with the environment than any previous pool of employees. They, for the most part, are weak in team efforts and use of systems to extend their own and the organizations functional ability. Much of their freedom and creativity has been at an individual and personal level and they have found few experiences which maintain their freedom, individuality and creativity while being part of an integrated team.

It can be said that the entertainer who draws no fans probably does not deserve them. The same is true of the manager / coach. Here we find the opportunity for another paradigm shift by tossing out the idea that, "because I like it and believe in it others should follow along". A belief that the employees owe nothing to the manager / coach which the manager / coach does not create will serve the future managers well. A belief that workers "should" do anything will just be a distraction and loss of leadership energy. The manager / coach who becomes focused on what is missing in the workplace will not find ways to lead it.

There is a loneliness of command, especially when there are few general or specific orders. One philosopher noted that one of God's worst tricks on mankind was to create man as a free moral agent rather than giving him the security of being pre-programmed like the other creatures. This experience is so frightening to most that they will give their freedom to the right cause. The cause, however, needs to be one that they have not previously found to be flawed.

Without the aid of a written handbook for organizational success, mixing the radically changing times, the Xers and the manager / coach can seem quite scary. This is especially true when some of the money, happiness and rewards are the property of the owner. It may be reassuring to the owner to know that broken paradigms have given us the forward pass, the helicopter, the jet engine, Air Jordan and Tiger Woods. Hopefully, we can identify the steps through which we tear down managerial paradigm paralysis and explore the essentials for effective managerial coaching. If the new role can be visualized, it can be achieved.

III

Visioning the Manager / Coach Model for the Future

ISSUES COVERED IN THIS CHAPTER.

- ◆ *Successful visions are essential but never rigid and static.*

- ◆ *The leader / manager learns from the employee.*

- ◆ *It is possible to know the essential variable of change without understanding all of the dynamics.*

- ◆ *Skills must be practiced daily in all life situations.*

- ◆ *There is potentially more power in having no power or direct control.*

- ◆ *Few people will cling to the anchor for security when offered a life preserver.*

- ◆ *The organization capable of the most made and executed decisions usually wins.*

- ◆ *Procrastination does not enhance effectiveness.*

- ◆ *Just do it! — Now.*

"When service delivery systems are seen as graduate management laboratories for the developing leader, the potential for training is unlimited."

Personal change without a vision is similar to taking a trip without a pre-determined destination or map to guide the process. Managerial visioning is as essential as it is to vision in sports, engineering, writing or art. The more specific and detailed the model for the desired behavior, the more obvious the steps for change will be.

The most successful managers of the future are faced with a need for change without a clear cut and available model for effecting that change. The situation is not unlike the predicament faced by women throughout the years. There is and has been a scarcity of female managerial models for women aspiring to higher management and leadership effectiveness. It has been necessary for most women to create a composite model from their experience with both male and female managers and their own fantasies. Managing the Xers is even a little more difficult. There are no readily available models to draw from for the visionary manager of the future. In fact, the envisioned model is in flux and may well be taught to the manager by the managed employees. Change will, of course, be more rapid when the student is more receptive and makes better use of changing information. "The teacher comes when the student is ready." Rigid and blind leaders / managers are slow learners.

Fortunately, there are steps which can help the student to be ready and invite the visit from the teacher. First, there must be a willingness to give up all past managerial approaches and to think reciprocally. A willingness to give up paradigms only require that they be validated not arbitrarily abandoned. The reverse thinking is especially important when it comes to the concept and exercise of power and authority. The old visions of authority and lines of authority will be replaced with insight into the essentials of indirect influence and guidance.

There is a story of Albert Switzer having been the change agent in the life of an intellectual atheist who became a devout Christian. When asked about what the good doctor had told him that inspired such great change, the changed man reported that he did not remember any specific discussion about religion issues.

One simple and readily available experience which will begin to open old paradigms to new managerial approaches can be provided through attempting the training of the house pet without the use of punishment or force. Another might be experienced through the proactive direction of a two year old. In each situation it is necessary to get attention, invite interaction, maintain focus, and influence behavior toward a pre-determined or developing goal. Such essence and influence requires total discipline and constant learning by the manager coach. *King Solomon's Ring* by Conrad Lorenz could be given as basic training regarding the ability to observe and use essential change variables.

Most skills abilities are enhanced with practice. The key to Generation X managerial leadership practice is to use common daily experiences as practice forums. This requires constant attention to the essential variables in the systems with which we interact. Attention development might include creating the exact service desired in a restaurant without making an issue or anyone at the table or the waitstaff being aware of the implicit direction being taken. When service delivery systems are seen as graduate management laboratories for the developing leader, the potential for training is unlimited. Anger and critical analysis tend to block insight, learning and personal essence.

Many manager / coaches are fortunate (or unfortunate) enough to be on one Board of Directors or another of an agency of non-profit group. In many cases this is an exercise in frustration as a result of the responsibility without any authority to make needed changes. This frustration is even more difficult in the political, religious and non-profit arenas. Yet, if we believe that there is potentially more power in no power, these situations provide maximum learning and growth opportunity for the manager of the future. Freud noted that neurosis, inadequacy and ineffectiveness only breed in secrecy. The art for this new breed of manager / coach will have to do with illuminating inadequacy and inefficiency without raising so much negativism that equally illuminated positive options will be rejected. Again, the goal is for optimal influence while having limited direct authority and power. People can come in off a limb if they do not have to admit being out on the limb in the first place.

Many manager/coaches become distracted by their own needs for affirmation and recognition for their position in the organization or to be seen as being "right." It takes a great deal of maturity to be in charge without having to have recognition. Leadership and managerial success will increasingly be reflective of power and influence which is not recognized or outwardly demonstrated. It is very difficult to resist a force that cannot be identified. " A man convinced against his will is of the same opinion still."

The personal decision making process provides another opportunity for management skill development. The ideal is to make all decisions with the least amount of information needed for an effective decision. Security oriented managers tend to do just the opposite and require an inordinate amount of information and other support to make decisions which should be obvious to them or certainly obvious with much less information than required. Their energies and process often has more to do with justification of position than with creative problem solving.

There is a common managerial illusion that there is more security in slow methodical decisions than in action on ones that are less than perfect. There is never a reason

to postpone a decision unless there is a very sound belief that additional information would bring forth a different decision. To paraphrase the poet Robert Burns— "there is no reason to stand around and agitate on the side if eventually you must swim the river."

The most successful organizations are the ones which make and execute the greatest number of decisions. The best Generation X manager / coach will exhibit the same characteristics. As you will remember, the Xers will respond best to the dynamic, fast paced and reality relevant organizational process. It is much like playing one on one basketball and betting all on yourself.

There are an unlimited number of sports examples which characterize the decision making and action style basic to Generation X management. Boxers, pitchers, quarterbacks and race car drivers make very rapid decisions which are almost spiritual in nature. They all describe being in a zone of interactive decision making that is outside of the cognitive process while it is actually happening. Cognitive involvement or any lack of trust in their intuitive ability only reduces performance at this level of involvement. The cognitive involvement, practice and direction occurred prior to the intentional action and habitual action of the intended behavior. This is not a new method. In fact, the Army calls this "Doing it by the numbers". With enough practice, the process becomes habitual. Many pets, wait persons and PTA meeting are basic to the point of being habitualized.

Few managers have the time to explore every detail of a situation prior to making a decision and / or choosing a direction. The goal is to use the least amount of information possible to make the best choices. Fortunately, there are many basic principles which are well known and can yield high probability for success with very limited amounts of specific information. Our limits are usually in the courage to act rather than in not knowing what to do.

An example would be that yielding to blackmail only encourages blackmail. It is not necessary to know all of the details to know that unless there are exceptional circumstances that one should not yield. The next question that arises has to do with the definition of exceptional. The answer is that there are darn few or that you are not dealing with a basic principle. The most identified "exceptional circumstance" is identified as such in the hope that there is a way of avoiding making the decision that the basic principle suggests. As noted earlier, examples of this are procrastination to avoid swimming the river and not taking responsibility for the repercussions of action.

Some other commonly accepted management principles include the need for consequences to occur very close to the inciting behavior and that most feedback to employees should be positive. In short, catch employees doing something positive, bring it to their attention immediately and regularly. Another would be to praise in public and criticize in private. Remember, criticism does not teach anyone to do anything.

Most manager / coaches, and individuals for that matter, are aware of what needs to be done to achieve success. Equally prevalent is the hesitation for actions in hopes that a larger, more comprehensive (or less painful) solution will magically appear. Unfortunately, those only come after we have handled those opportunities of which we are aware. Doing so often leads to the evaporation of the larger issues which need magical solutions. Air Jordan and Nike suggest "Just do it!". "Now" might be added to the slogan for us all.

Hopefully this chapter has given some illumination to the suggested nature of the manager of Generation X. The authors have tried to describe the tasks of the manager and the skills associated with providing direction, motivation and behavioral focus with only limited control or real authority. It is, of course, the daily practice in multiple and diverse settings which provide the basic skills and confidence to quickly trust the intuitive with only limited information. The athletic models should provide some examples of the performance levels and rewards which "Zone" performance can yield.

· · NOTES · ·

IV

High Maintenance For High Performance

Issues covered in this chapter.

♦ *The importance of personal attention.*

♦ *The essentials of a strong relationship.*

♦ *Constant improvement keeps the organizational process from becoming static.*

♦ *"No Huddle" management.*

♦ *Rid the organization of too many sacred cows.*

♦ *Allow focus to become an obsession.*

♦ *Never lower the bar. The Xer must have challenge.*

♦ *Raise expectations and watch the Xer blossom.*

Personal attention must be paid. Both personal and attention equal in importance, but both are essential for high performance from the Xers. With a long standing distrust of authority and official roles, relationship is the big contact between the Xer and the manager / coach.

Xers, remember, are very bright and somewhat suspicious because of their experience with society's many facades. Relationships with Xers must be real, in depth and person to person, never role to role. The story line of the developing relationship with the Xer must be retained and appropriately reflected upon. There must be attention and care but the interaction must be remembered for its content, support and direction.

There is always a mutual sharing in any real interaction. The constant interchange includes goals, dreams, intensity, familiarity, information and hobbies. The Xer insists on the respect of being related to as a person prior to just being an employee. The successful manager / coach finds that the personal relationship breeds a trust which enhances communication, good will and a willingness or desire to please and perform all toward the goal of having the relationship "work out". Mission accomplished. A good relationship will cover a lot of mistakes before they happen.

The need for and power of relationships has always been recognized. It is more important with the Xers because there is very limited authority, power or force on which to fall back. When cooperative effectiveness is not achieved through a well defined relationship, there is little upon which the team may rely. The higher and more

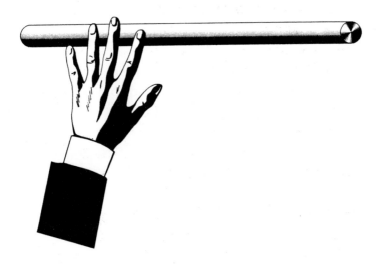

meaningful the shared goals of the relationship, the stronger the relationship will be.

Xers will respond to challenge if it is real, worthwhile and in some way will yield a sense of elitism. The Xers are not unique in their desire to be unique, special and good at what they do. The manager / coach has the individuals of the team each understanding and able to visualize just how they are to be special. This is where the quality, methods, time and cost of what is to be done can be used effectively. Constant improvements also have the potential to challenge.

As we have noted before, the Xers will also assist the manager / coach in growth. It is just as important for the manager / coach to keep focus on and share personal goals and growth steps as it is for them to ask for them. Xers seem to thrive in an open environment where there are few secrets and everyone's performance and investment is common knowledge. This open environment uses individual and group dynamics to do what most of the conventional managers are required to handle. The Xer feels honored when a manager / coach changes approach to an Xer's input.

The responsibility of the leader of the Xers is to maintain the focus of what needs to be done, not how it is to be done. The leader is a cheer leader, a motivator, a model and a feed back specialist. In the best of situations, the leader is actually aware of the team and individual performance and is constantly helping to explore options

for continued growth and improvement. Boredom is removed when the way in which everything operates is constantly challenged.

The demand for constant improvement leads to a challenge for constant and individual growth. This is where the relationship developed with each team member becomes crucial. We are asking them to step out of their comfort zones just as we do and for us to jointly try new behavior with new and uncharted outcomes. It is difficult to take this trip with someone you do not trust. Individual and organizational growth plans cannot be cut into stone. In effect, it is always necessary to follow opportunities. In other words, always run toward daylight. The fear of uncertainty and risk cannot win and lead to static organizational process.

Xers are bright and can understand overriding concepts if they are properly presented. Often the foundation concepts and principles are the only support for immediate action available to the employee or leader. The security given by understanding the concepts and principles gives the Xers the opportunity for quick action and success beyond their years of experience. When this occurs, we have decisions and activities occurring at the lowest possible level of the organization and having success. Xers need more concepts and principles while having fewer concrete repetitions.

Xers are used to thirty minute television programs where things happen quickly. The channel will be changed even if a thirty minute movie is not moving rapidly enough. The same happens to fights, ballgames and even car races. Most of us, especially the Xers, will not tolerate a slow pace. Here we are truly talking about "no huddle" management. The Xer will teach management the importance of time.

Admittedly, it is difficult to bring excitement, constant change and immediate reward into some types of widget making. Frequent proactive change can be brought to the organization through the use of cross training and job sharing. These needed challenges and opportunities through orienting the organization toward the team concept and shifting the responsibility in the organization to a vertical one. Every process, concept and approach should face being tried another way. There should, as well, be few sacred cows beyond these four:

> IMMEDIACY
> COST EFFECTIVENESS
> QUALITY
> SAFETY.

The organizational commitment to Xers should be that either we give every opportunity to grow or we will help

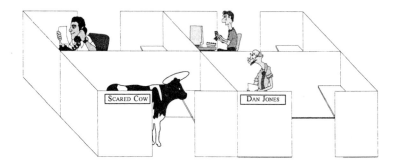

you to find a place where you can self actualize. "It would be irresponsible of our organization to hold you hostage and prevent you from following your dream." It is equally irresponsible for us to not offer you a better dream which is advantageous to us both. Remember, no deal is a good deal unless it is to the advantage to all concerned.

Focus guides attention and gives meaning. Professionals in all arenas are obsessed with keeping focus. A golfer will meditate prior to each shot. Football teams on the sideline during the game will receive a fax from the control booth where coaches have photographed the opposing team, studied possible options and sent recommendations on weakness down to the coach. Comedians will also use a video tape of their performance to give vital feedback to help them focus on the elements needed for success. Management information systems which give daily and hourly performance feedback are basic to the world class performance experience which is the goals of the Xers. Remember, the required life experiences will lead the Xer on a steamer trip to the Horn of Africa or a trip on the Appalachian Trail if work pace is not stimulating enough. Pilots rely on a variety of information feedback to maintain an exact focus on their course and position. Xers love this sort of feedback. They like to know how many, what quality, what profit and what response from the customers.

Again, an obsession with focus only pushes the leader / coach to have the vision and discipline to provide an organizational, a personal and an individual employee with focus. If the leader is unable to maintain focus on essential variables, then it is likely that the entire process will deteriorate from there.

A focus on fun is one of the essential variables most commonly avoided or lost entirely. The fun comes from how we do things and with what attitude, not what we are doing. This has been previously noted. After all, it is difficult to believe that we can get too serious about making most widgets, especially those used and worshipped by the teens. However, those who have seen the movie, *The Sting* can realize the excitement from seeing any intentional process come together in a productive and desired manner. Making things happen is always an exciting experience.

High performance expectations are another foundation for high individual and group motivation. This, of course, is not unique to the Xers. It is rather universal to all individual and group performance. Few people like to do anything that they do not do well. It is embarrassing. It is especially embarrassing to not be able to do some mundane task well. The converse is true. Excitement can be found even in the most mundane activity if done at a world class level.

Shared high performance has long been known to be an even stronger motivator than solo activities. There seems to be an affirmation of each individual's performance when seen as part of a shared experience. A hole-in-one is exciting, but even more so when it wins for the team or brings excitement when seen by other people. A hole-in-one is less fulfilling and almost an empty experience when playing solo.

Xers can become especially dedicated when they choose to be part of a high performance team. The successful manager is able to have the entire team perform above the past experiences of the individuals involved. Group synergism occurs when the needs of the individuals to belong are met.

The worst approach to an Xer is to lower either group or individual performance goals. This approach to ineffectiveness just takes away value from the entire work experience which may have been marginal in the beginning. It is important to remember that Xers respond to challenge and elitism. The higher the risk and greater the challenge, the more enthusiasm shown by the Xer.

The Xer has a low frustration tolerance, and it is important to avoid failure or poor performance if possible.

1978

HBO

Disco

Station Wagons

8-track tapes

Hand Held Calculators

IBM Selectric

For this reason, if for no other, a very close relationship with frequent reality checks is important. If there is a problem, it is the coach's responsibility to find a solution for success. Xers do not take criticism well.

Attention can be given through training, novel approaches and even shared attempts at finding a way to conquer this "turkey." Fixing blame on a person rather than the problem will always be destructive and distract from the systems and managerial deficiencies. Employees can assist in problem solving if they are not dodging criticism.

Possibly the best approach to improving lagging Xer performance is to raise the standard and jointly plan with the Xer for some magical and high-yield approach to the problem. Xers love the challenge and are bright enough to create something as effective as it is probably destructive to conventional paradigms. Here again the Xer tends to train the manager / coach as much as the manager / coach trains the Xer.

1998

CELLULAR PHONES

MINI-SATELLITE DISHES

LIFE ON MARS

PERSONAL COMMUTATIONS SERVICES (PCS)

COMPACT LASER DISCS

FIBER OPTICS

HAND HELD COMPUTERS

The most exciting aspect of the Xers is their ability to see the solutions which transcend both conventional approaches and what seem to be the rational laws. Who would have ever believed in the cellular phone, fax, FedEx or plastic cars twenty years ago? If it already exists, it is most probably obsolete. The Xer, in almost all cases, has a better chance of finding a better way than the Owner / Manager. They live outside of the existing envelope of conventional thinking.

The smallest prizes in life are often the most fun and exciting for people. Cracker Jack found this gimmick effective in selling over-priced popcorn. Coca Cola and Publisher's Clearing House have also used this idea. Xers love the intrigue of prizes, and it is important to remember that random reinforcement or prizes are more powerful than regular, predictable "goodies." Money is good, but not the most important compensation to the Xer.

There is an old golfer's joke that a one iron held high above the head would protect from lightening, because, "even God can't hit a one iron." Recently, it has been found that a club similar to the one iron may well be the longest hitting of all golf clubs. The Xers may be the one iron for employee effectiveness. Who would ever have thought of that possibility.

• • NOTES • •

· · NOTES · ·

V

Paradigm Busters

ISSUES COVERED IN THIS CHAPTER.

- ◆ *Successful management requires innovative, out of the box thinking.*

- ◆ *Self actualization within the organization is the strongest motivator.*

- ◆ *There is real joy in paradigm busting, especially when paradigms fall in all aspects of life.*

- ◆ *Don't let strong profits stifle creativity. Strong leaders know the next step and are excited.*

- ◆ *Xers will follow the enthusiastic risk taker.*

- ◆ *A successful leader must be a maverick.*

Successful Xer management requires constant attention to the creative possibilities for improving manufacturing or service process and empowering employees. Xers respect knowledgeable, competent and flexible leaders. As has been noted before, the Xer responds to mutuality in a relationship rather than to loyalty for an organization. Self actualization and recognition are the highest motivators.

The manager's creative investigations have the greatest possible yield when they are big, hairy, bodacious or otherwise unorthodox. Anything within the ordinary tends to be a part of an existing comfort zone and can give only arithmetic addition rather than the exciting quantum changes needed. Xers like the big bang even if connected to significant risk. In addition, therein lies some of the limits most managers of the Xers face. Again, the Xer has something to teach the manager / coach.

Xers are under-consumers and, often, do not have a lot to lose. Therefore, they are not fearful of risk. The managers or coaches of the Xers are often Baby Boomers who are much more establishment-oriented and rather acquisitive. Since they have more to risk, they are more conservative. To the Xer, this approach to anything has the same affect as an old, slow-paced movie. They get bored and want to change the channel. The approach gives the illusion of security while raising risks.

It is important to remember that the Xer is intelligent, well-read and has had a lot of exposure to high tech thinking. They are aware that there are many different ways to approach almost anything. Gadgets, paradoxical solutions and paradigm busters fascinate them. Electric cars, waterless toilets, recycling and ecologically sensitive approaches excite them. Xers love to transcend society with different approaches. It is even better if the approaches are more effective.

The Xer is suspicious of the establishment and holds little respect for anything that the society has created. Years of experience with the paralysis of our educational, legal, and governing systems has led them to know that there has to be another way or "it" really does not matter anyway. They know that our sacred jury system with its foundation in being tried by randomly selected peers really means a jury that has been manipulated and contaminated by the most creative of lawyers. Truth and justice are seldom either the issue or the focus of legal actions.

Paradigm busting can be forced, but creativity is not usually that easy. In most cases, it is easier to see creative change opportunity in someone else's process. The real joy in the busting process comes when one does it consistently in all situations from the laundry, restaurant, the airline or the crowd control at the ball park. Paradigm-busting thinking can and should become a way of life for the manager of the next century.

Constant challenge of the thinking basic to processes which are not familiar and in which our perceptual interpretations have not become fixed will eventually lead to spontaneous insights into the familiar and into areas where there is personal paradigm paralysis. Any movement away from habit is good practice for the growing manager. A change in what, where, how we eat breakfast, play golf or approach family activities will stimulate changes in our personal problem-solving approaches.

Security, excessive time, strong profits and limited competition are all very supportive of habit and paradigm paralysis. Unfortunately, all of the above are more characteristic of the managers of the Xers than of the Xers themselves. It is in the interchange around these variables of security and complacency regarding time, profits and respect for affluence that the Xers will begin to train their managers. It is not an easy training experience for either. It will be, however, exciting and extremely productive for both. It is difficult to be lazy in a high performance learning environment, especially if that environment is also fun.

The belief that there is real security and the constant search for it blinds those searching to the many opportunities for increased creativity and productivity which are the nearest true things to security. The creative, innovative, flexible and productive people and organizations always seem to have a better life experience than those who fiercely try to protect obsolete equipment, goods and processes. It is easy to find nature's least dynamic creatures. They are the ones with the skills and other external protection.

Ownership of capital equipment is expensive and can lead to holding on to obsolete equipment. Old or obsolete equipment is frequently the cornerstone for obsolete production and decision making. It is the effective use of capital goods which leads to success, not the ownership of those goods. Movement and change are much more rapid when the company is not dragging along heavy

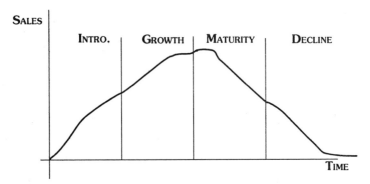

The time to be creative, do the strategic planning and prepare for change is when profits are good.

capital investments. Ownership is best when there is an expectation of appreciation and there is an extended life expectancy for all concrete possessions. The art of management has a lot to do with knowing when to write off and run. Hopefully, the run will be into the first wave of a new generation of efficiency and productivity.

Strong profits can be the strongest sedative of all. Many managers find it impossible to even think about the position of their company or product in its life cycle when profits are strong and energies are dedicated to production or service. Labor Day is the best sales day at some beaches. There is often free beer on the day after Labor Day. The successful manager always has the foundations for the next step prepared and is excitingly sharing it with the team.

All products and most companies have life cycles. The time to be creative, do the strategic planning and prepare for change is when profits are good. Urgency increases and funds for change decrease on the down slope of the life cycle. In addition, the availability of alternatives may well have passed.

It is the acute awareness of the lack of permanence or security that breeds the Xers lack of loyalty to the establishment and organizations. The manner in which management proactively deals with the challenges of change invites Xer loyalty, motivation and devotion. The Xers will follow those who attack, with enthusiasm, situations which will again bring uncertainty in their lives. They love the experience of power over or courage in the face of intrusions.

The authors' theory that the successful Xer manager must become somewhat of a renegade is likely clear by now. This manager must excel in spite of situations rather than because of support given by the existing situation. Risk takers, innovators and rapid decision makers will be rewarded by Xer performance and loyalty.

· · NOTES · ·

VI

Never Have So Few Achieved So Much

ISSUES COVERED IN THIS CHAPTER:

- *Efficiency is ever increasing for the strong managers and companies.*
- *The key to future success is in the ability to transcend existing paradigms.*
- *Change happens to all in all situations.*
- *Courageous leaders manage and operate without a lot of support using the moral compass.*
- *Maslow's Hierarchy of Needs points us toward self actualization.*

> ## "And you all know,
> ## security is mortals'
> ## chiefest enemy"
> —Shakespeare, *Macbeth*,
> Act III Scene 5.

Efficiency has to do with how little human and capital energy it takes to do anything. There is no question about the increased efficiency in every aspect of manufacturing and service delivery. We are living in the most efficient and productive period in history. The demand for efficiency will likely begin to receive the same attention previously given to quality. Many long cherished approaches, tools, systems and paradigms have long since been obsolete. They are dead, just not buried.

It was once said that managers were useless if the work force had enough time and resources to accomplish the task. Managers and systems are essential when there is time, budget and resource restrictions. Brains and brash have to be used to replace brawn. Managers who require the least amount of time and the fewest number of workers to excel will be the ones written about. David handled Goliath by breaking the paradigm. The union management can bring General Motors to a stop with a strategically chosen strike at a relatively small component parts operation. A commando unit can achieve what a large invasion would have a difficult time with. These are all examples of highly efficient operations, all of which could be classified as paradigm busters.

The Xers have distrust in the existing social establishment paradigms for many reasons. They have had uncertainty and disillusionment visited upon them because of the paradigm. The successful Xer manager / leader will gradually have the same lack of respect for the paradigms which control and limit society, but their distrust will come from a different perspective. The paradigms are clumsy, ineffective and, in most cases, a joke. The successful manager / coach will be asked to give up something, a paradigm, that has served him / her well in the past.

Atomic weapons are obsolete. Everyone that has them as well as the equipment to deliver them is extremely reluctant to use them. Those most likely to use the weapons of mass destruction have ready access to and the delivery capabilities for equally destructive biological weapons with volunteers ready to deliver them. Yet, the western economy is heavily rooted in and dependant upon an obsolete illusion of security.

The chaos which has stifled the Xers is seen as fertile opportunity for the leader / manager. Opportunity always abides in chaos. As the enlightened Xer manager finally accepts that there is no security and takes the entrepreneurial approach to relating to chaos, the Xer leader / manager becomes more Xer than the Xers themselves. This enlightened approach can occur just as actively in a large corporation as in a small, independently owned organization. The key is in the transcendence of existing cultural and structural paradigms.

With a dedication to the thesis that change happens to all in all situations, there is little energy wasted in resisting change. All energy goes to attempts to move with, influence and / or guide the change. Hopefully, to get on top of the wave and ride it in.

Elitism and success always tend to bring rejection from the masses. It is much easier to reduce personal anxiety by restructuring the creative change in others than it is to make the personal changes needed to remain competitive. Therefore, effective and creative leadership / management for the Xers may well be "only for the lonely". It may be better said, "only for those willing to risk trying it alone."

> *"The reasonable man adapts himself to the world; the unreasonable one persists in trying to adapt the world to himself. Therefore, all progress depends upon the unreasonable man."*
> —Excerpt from *The Revolutionist Handbook* by George Bernard Shaw.

In addition to having to be willing to go forth and manage without a great deal of support, the leader / manager is asked to do so without any real road map or general orders. The situation is not unlike the situation facing captains of the old British Empire sailing fleet. "Go forth to X latitude and X longitude and act in the best interests of the Queen." Such situation certainly provides a great deal of freedom and opportunity for flexibility, but with only limited support. As alluded to earlier, it is said that God's greatest dirty trick was to make man a free moral agent. Free to chose his own course.

There is good news for the enlightened leader / manager. As previously noted, the answers are readily available and, in fact, known to most of those on the team. There is even better news. Those answers not readily available came into awareness when the available ones are acted upon. Vision is lost when there is not enough courage to bring action appropriate to the vision. The security of the familiar and comfortable is a great blinder to the enlightenment.

Cancer is so dangerous because it starts out as a normal cell and is not detected by the body's immune system until it has gotten so far developed that it is beyond the power of most immune systems. The leader / manager that adopts and extends Xer thinking is not seen as an outside invader and, in fact, becomes cherished as a guide to the movement.

The question here has to do with the goals, objectives and end purpose of the movement. Fortunately, we have Maslow's Hierarchy of Needs to guide us. In short, Maslow said that as soon as the basic needs are met, the individual seeks first to have a group of significant others of high purpose and then move toward self actualization. Interestingly enough, the goals and end products, the needs of Generation Mature, the Boomers and the Xers are all the same. There are different routes for the trip. However, the Xers have the best chance for the highest success with

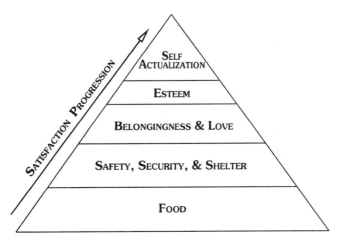

In an affluent society, food, water and shelter are available for most people. The real motivation is seen in providing belonging and ultimately self actualization.

proper leaders / managers. Without them, they will also get there. It will just take longer and be more painful for everyone involved.

The potentials for future products and efficiencies for both goods and services in this country are fantastic. The labor crunch is wonderful. It will only push for the creative leadership / management suggested by the authors. Our entire labor force will be more effective as we go. The limited availability of workers is not unlike lowering the water level in a pond. Only a few inches will show where the rocks are. A labor shortage will illuminate other approaches.

Thank God for the Xers!

Summary

The purpose of the book has been to illuminate and champion one of our country's greatest ever resources, Generation X. This group, born in the 1960's and 1970's has been given very mixed reviews. Some see them as a breath of fresh air and others feel that they cannot be controlled and are destructive to all that is sacred.

The authors contend that the group is brighter, better educated, more flexible and capable of achievements beyond the imaginations of previous generations. Freedom from many of the controlling and limiting paradigms of the society gives the Xers the ability to move more rapidly, take more risks and to effectively interact in the information society.

The extra ordinary achievement will, however, be largely rooted in older leaders / managers who are more entrepreneurial and Xer than members of Generation X themselves. These new style managers will use personal relationships, elitist visions and high performance expectations to bring in the motivating variable basic to all. As most basic needs are met in an affluent society, emphasis will be on empowerment for individuals and small, high performance teams. Self actualization will be held sacred by all and the manager / leader will be expected to go first. Modeldom by the leader / manager will take the place of the old time goddess martyrdom.

The future is brighter than ever for those having the courage.

"Forget likes and dislikes. Do what must be done. That is not happiness, that is greatness."
—George Bernard Shaw.

The Authors

Don Boone, MSW

Don has more than thirty years experience as a professional in human performance development. He has both business and counseling degrees and has taught at several universities throughout the United States.

Don's existential approach to life and work is very simple, practical and demanding and has been very successful in a wide range of settings. Generation-X and managers who work along side of them are finding the existential principles and approaches to be especially rewarding.

Asheville, North Carolina has always been home for Don. However, he has business interests in California and travels extensively.

Donna Boone Martin, MBA

Donna Boone Martin has an MBA (Master of Business Administration) degree from the University of Tennessee at Knoxville. Donna brings a marketing perspective to this book, having been involved in corporate marketing in both small and large international companies. Currently, Martin is CEO of HES Management Consultants, specializing in designing and implementing marketing and operating systems for family and independently-owned businesses.

Daniel B. Martin III

Dan Martin has more than fifteen years experience in Business Management, Business Communications and Business Development. His early career began in the newspaper industry; however, most of his experience has been gained as an integral member of the booming telecommunications industry. Dan has led his companies to record profits and cash flows by helping to break the old mold and finding new ways to achieve success. Dan believes that success can be achieved when, as mangers, we ask, "Why?" and, if the answer is not there, blaze a new trail. This philosophy makes for better employees, provides stellar customer service, and can effect a fundamental change in business.

Dan brings a "nuts and bolts" business perspective to HES Management Consultants. Dan is a native of Texas, but now lives, works, and plays in Asheville, North Carolina.

· · NOTES · ·

· · NOTES · ·

Other Publications Available From:

16 Spears Ave. #2
Asheville, N.C. 28801
Phone (828) 258-0905
Fax (828) 252-6294

Alternatives to Alcoholism's Grand Conspiracy
— Don Boone, MSW — 1-56664-001-6 — **WorldComm®** 6.95

This controversial book explodes myths about substance abuse and offers workable alternatives. 64 pages, 5.5x8.5

The Courage to Manage (2nd Ed)
— D. Boone & others — 1-56664-090-3 — **WorldComm®** 9.95

Emphasis on family and personal planning of business concerns. Helpful, inspirational methods of business management. 100 pages, trade paper, b&w illustrations.

Creative Loving
— Don Boone, MSW — 1-56664-064-4 — **WorldComm®** 9.95

A handbook dedicated to optimism and hope for the chronically mentally ill and their families. Chronic mental illness can be treated. Disabled individuals can become effective. The family is a primary treatment tool. 6x9, 64 pages.

Family Business in the Family Business
— Don Boone & Donna Martin — 1-56664-115-2 — **WorldComm®** 9.95

The family business model was the first business model and continues to be the most effective management model. This book helps the reader realize the rich potential of a family business and avoid the many pitfalls. Small but mighty book! Paper, 76 pages.

The Myth That Kills
— Don Boone, MSW — 1-56664-117-9 — **WorldComm®** 9.95

This book offers new hope to those suffering from alcohol and other types of addictions. In direct, readable language, it explodes myths about the treatment of substance abuse and offers workable alternatives. 5.5x8.5, 76 pages, illustrated.

Personal Options for Organizational Change
— Boone & Martin — 1-56664-096-2 — **WorldComm®** 9.95

Surviving or thriving, change is inevitable while growth is optional and stress is a choice. A handbook for creating your own experience and for thriving in this complicated and changing world. 6x9, 64 pages.

You Chi: The Healing Spirit
— Don Boone, MSW & Laura Boone, RN — 1-56664-048-2 —
WorldComm® 9.95

This personal guide to "Living in Spite of Cancer" helps the reader become an informed participant in the recovery process. 6x9, 80 pages.